Jo,

Hod 12/11

1

Instant Insights on...

Defining Moments with Family, Friends, & More

LESIA ZABLOCKIJ, ACC

Instant Insights on ...
Defining Moments with Family, Friends, & More
By Lesia Zablockij, ACC

Copyright © 2017 by Lesia Zablockij, ACC

All rights reserved. No part of this publication may be reproduced, distributed, or transmitted in any form or by any means, including photocopying, recording, or other electronic or mechanical methods, or by any information storage and retrieval system, without the prior written permission of the publisher and author, except in the case of brief quotations embodied in critical reviews and certain other non-commercial uses permitted by copyright law.

Crescendo Publishing, LLC
300 Carlsbad Village Drive
Ste. 108A, #443
Carlsbad, California 92008-2999

www.CrescendoPublishing.com
GetPublished@CrescendoPublishing.com
1-877-575-8814

ISBN: 978-1-944177-69-0 (P)
ISBN: 978-1-944177-70-6 (E)

Printed in the United States of America
Cover design by Melody Hunter

10 9 8 7 6 5 4 3 2 1

What You Will Learn in This Book

We all have relationships. Whether they are family, friends, coworkers, significant others, or a myriad of other types of relationships, we all have them.

Author Lesia Zablockij takes you on a journey through several types of relationships, each one reaching a point she refers to as a "defining moment." In these instances, a defining moment is a turning point in each relationship. They have reached a fork in the road and can go in any direction from that point.

Throughout our lives, we are tested in our relationships. Those challenges continue to show up until we find a way to come to terms with the lessons we need to learn.

Because the author has experienced her own challenges, she has a vantage point from which to help others. She realized being open to looking at things from a new perspective was often helpful. Assuming that one version of a specific situation is the correct one, or even the only one, is believing that side is the only truth. Looking at the situation from a new angle can provide much insight and open us up to new information and possibilities. With a new perspective, the way you handle relationships could change, making it easier to move forward and make different choices.

In this book, you'll get ***Instant Insights*** on ...

- Recognizing defining moments in relationships

- Seeing the results of a defining moment

- Learning new defining moments are possible and allowing for different outcomes

- Witnessing that some relationships are fleeting while others are concrete

- Discovering the importance of the longest relationship you will ever have

- Awareness is key

- Acceptance is mandatory

- New choices are always available

A Gift from the Author

To help you gain some awareness into your relationships, the author is happy to provide you with the following **bonus** gifts that she hopes will inspire and help you:

- A copy of her first book, Soul Fire Café, Making Peace with the One in the Mirror is available in ebook format at www.SoulFireCafe.com

- A step-by-step workbook to help you create more rewarding relationships in your future; just e-mail the author at: AlteringMindsets@gmail.com and write "send workbook" in the subject line.

Dedication

Felicia Zablockij – A beautiful soul taken much too soon. She touched so many. She had a way of being honest and telling people the truth without judging or criticizing. It was just stated as a fact and not meant to ever hurt or belittle anyone.

One of my favorite memories is when Felicia watched a friend of mine carry out her morning beauty regimen. Felicia sat, watched, and commented, "You sure put a lot of stuff on your face." My friend asked Felicia if it made a difference, to which Felicia replied, "Not really" and she giggled. That was her way!

Felicia taught us all about relationships. She loved unconditionally and just wanted to be loved back, and she was—by so many. She understood about boundaries, and if you crossed hers or if you were just being silly or unreasonable, she would make no bones about letting you know, but never in a way that hurt anyone. She would just call you out on your bullshit and then move on. She was done, and there should be no hard feelings.

She took care of her friends, her family, and her pets. Felicia taught us all well!

Felicia: The part in our hearts you so gently touched will always glow when we think of you. Much love, our girl. You will be missed forever.

Table of Contents

Friendships

I believe in supporting someone I consider my friend. That means I listen when I need to, I help when someone wants my help, and I try to keep my opinions to myself during those times when I realize I should (which is hopefully more often than not, but sometimes I do slip!).

I also hope that I will get that in return, but it's not always the case. It's important to note that hope is very different from expectation. I hope that I will get that in return, but expecting to get it is not really accepting the person for who they are. Expectation is more like wanting your friend to be who you think they should be and wanting their actions to be consistent with your ideas. Nobody needs to live by your ideals, but a true friend will understand them.

People are made up of their own stories and life experiences. Everyone has hardships in their lives, and you may have no clue what they are or that they even exist. If you have an expectation about how someone should behave as "repayment" for your friendship, you are doing something with conditions, and that is no longer a friendship. It seems more like a bargaining chip people are using with each other: If I do this for you, then I expect you will do the same for me. They key word here is "use," and true friends do not "use" each other.

Friendships only flourish if both sides work at it. You can't make a friendship exist if only one party is participating and making the effort to keep the relationship going. You both have to be equally committed. I was told once that the phone rings both ways. Don't wait for the other person to make a move. Once you make the move, you will find out what's truly going on and will no longer have to wonder as you will have the answer. If you don't make the move, it's like waiting for a diagnosis—waiting, wondering, speculating, and coming up with all kinds of crazy scenarios. It's just not worth wasting your time.

If a friendship is changing, it may be time to see if you can figure out why and whether those changes can be integrated so that the friendship can continue. If it's been a strong friendship, then it is worth finding out what's happening. Take the time. Make the effort. See what happens. If it is time to part ways—even temporarily—then you can do so without the stories that get created in your head and without hard feelings. It's easier to reunite in the future if there are no bad feelings in the way.

If you have reached this point in your friendship, you may have reached a defining moment that could change the basis of the friendship forever.

It may be time to create a new defining moment that may return the friendship to what it was or what you want it to be instead of plowing down the path to a friendship neither one of you may want. If you sense a change in your friendship, start a conversation and openly figure out what is changing and why.

The potential for a new defining moment and the creation of a stronger friendship may be worth being vulnerable to see what went awry. Strong friendships are few and far between. Remember that friendship means supporting each other even when it's ugly and hard. If you have strong friendships in your life, cherish those relationships. Work through the bumps. You may surprise yourselves by coming out stronger at the other end.

Life happens and daily pressures can make us a little self-absorbed. We veer off track and sometimes unintentionally hurt others or do things that someone else may perceive as unusual. Assumptions are made that may or may not be true, and the tangled web begins.

I was told many years ago that if you make it through your life with one true and trusted friend, you are very lucky. I always remember that when issues come up with friends. If it's worth saving, have the conversation. Leave your preconceived notions at the door and have an honest discussion to uncover what may really be going on. Figure out how you may have gotten off track. You might just uncover something you never knew. You may find out it had nothing to do with you, even though you thought it was all about you (as we sometimes do). A good friend is sometimes just a safe place to let go of pain. That's the price of friendship.

Your Instant Insights...

- Friendships only flourish if both sides work at it. You can't make a friendship exist if only one party is participating and making the effort to keep the relationship going.

- Take the time. Make the effort. See what happens. If it is time to part ways—even temporarily—then you can do so without the stories that get created in your head and without hard feelings.

- Work through the bumps. You may surprise yourselves by coming out stronger at the other end.

Friends at Crossroads

Lily and Ava had been friends for many years. Lily welcomed her friends to get to know each other, and over the years, Ava got to know Lily's family and friends. All of Lily's friends and family attended events together, and it was always a welcoming group environment. That was the way Lily liked it. She was proud of her family and proud of her friends. Everyone was always welcome, no matter what the event. The more the merrier.

At one point, there was a break in Lily's family dynamic, and it caused a great deal of discord and hurt feelings. Relationships ended, and others suffered. It was all unnecessary, but people felt the need to stand their ground, even if that ground was shaky.

Ava had been included in many relationships because of Lily; however, Lily was surprised that Ava continued on with a couple of these relationships after they ended with Lily. Because Lily felt Ava was being disloyal to her, she had difficulty accepting it. What made it harder was

Ava continually tried to find ways to heal the relationships and reunite everybody. Lily felt she was always defending her actions, explaining that there are two sides to any relationship and that both sides have to want to try to heal the rift. Neither side was interested as it was a relationship that no longer existed because of familial disconnections.

The continuous discussions about the situation frustrated Lily because she didn't feel she could get through to Ava, who thought there had to be a way to mend the fences. She wouldn't let up trying to come up with a solution. Lily felt forced to try to explain her position over and over again. It almost cost them their friendship.

Lily was hurt that Ava had formed an allegiance with these people. She felt Ava hadn't been supportive of her, and it brought into question their relationship of many years. In time, Lily let go of her negative feelings about who Ava continued to see, but a line had to be drawn in the sand. In the future, Ava was not to discuss these other people with Lily, and she was not to discuss Lily's private affairs with the others. It was not an easy solution, but it was the only way they could maintain their friendship.

A defining moment in their friendship came when Lily finally understood that Ava would never fully comprehend what happened with the other people in Lily's life. Lily understood Ava meant no malice by constantly trying to create new bonds among all the parties. Lily had to accept that Ava just wouldn't get it. On Ava's part, she had to understand that Lily wanted no part of her life shared with these estranged people and didn't want to hear about their lives either. On rare occasions, the line was crossed, but it was never open for discussion or commentary, and that was how they were able to move forward.

If someone has been blessed to have lived a life with limited exposure to tumultuous relationships, it is difficult for them to understand the positions that each party feels the need to take. Stepping back and understanding it through each other's eyes is, in some instances, the only way to save a friendship.

Life can be hard, and tough times exist, some of which cannot be overlooked or explained. Accepting this can help keep a friendship alive instead of trying to convince both sides that it needs to be fixed. Sometimes there is just no reason to fix some relationships, nor any interest in doing so. It's not even a matter of time passing to allow healing. It's about both sides having the desire and commitment to do what needs to be done, and not everybody has that sense of commitment or that desire.

Realizing that a person cannot control who another person associates with is important and sometimes a difficult pill to swallow. Even if it hurts, there are ways to work around it. The key is both parties have to want to maintain their friendship. When you look at the benefits of keeping a friendship together, only you can decide whether or not it's worth it to overlook choices that may not make you happy.

Your Instant Insights...

- Stepping back and understanding an event through each other's eyes is, in some instances, the only way to save a friendship.

- Sometimes there is just no reason to fix some relationships, nor is there an interest in doing so.

- The key is both parties have to want to maintain their friendship.

Opening Your Home

Years ago, Rhonda and Tammy had been friends until Rhonda moved away. One day, circumstances made Tammy move closer to Rhonda. Rhonda was thrilled to renew the friendship and to be able to help Tammy adjust to her new life and surroundings. Although they still didn't live in the same city, they were closer and could visit often.

Davis, Tammy's husband, travelled into the city regularly for meetings and training. When the weather turned, travelling back home could become a little treacherous with the icy roads and low visibility. Rhonda and Jay were always happy to help in any way they could, so they extended an invitation to Davis for him to overnight at their home when the weather was bad. Davis readily accepted the invitation.

Jocelyn, a friend of Rhonda and Jay, was a little stunned to hear of the invitation, knowing that her friends liked the peacefulness of their home and their time together, but because it was none of her business, she kept it to herself.

Sometimes when an outside party voices their concern, it can harm the relationship. Maybe it could help, but it could also make the outside party lose out, regardless of the intent to not injure and to simply point something out. Sometimes you have to sit back, watch it play out, and be there for support afterwards, if needed.

As time went on, it seemed that instead of occasionally staying overnight due to the weather, Davis began spending the weekday evenings at their home. There was no discussion; he just assumed that it was fine because he was invited to stay.

The situation became uncomfortable. Rhonda and Jay felt like Davis was taking advantage of them, and it was turning into a bad situation. Davis took the opportunity to participate in other things later into the evening because he didn't have to drive back home. That wasn't the intended arrangement. They didn't sign up for a roommate. He would come in late, and the door alarm would beep and wake up Rhonda and Jay who got up early for work.

Davis seemed to have a lack of respect for Rhonda and Jay. He didn't see that their invitation was offered as a favor so that he wouldn't have to drive on bad roads. It became an expectation on his part, and resentment began to grow as Rhonda and Jay felt taken for granted. Davis always left his boots at the door instead of putting them away, and Rhonda and Jay would trip over them. It was as if he was oblivious that he was the guest and not a fellow roommate.

The final straw came one day when it was snowing. Jay came home to find his wife outside shoveling the snow while Davis relaxed in the house. Davis had walked right past her and didn't even think to offer to help her with the shoveling.

The defining moment in the relationship was when it could no longer be ignored that Davis felt he was entitled to stay at their house, rather than appreciating the favor that was extended to him to make his life easier and keep him safe. Sadly, it ended up ruining a good friendship with Tammy as well.

Tammy, of course, sided with her husband, and although the offer to help was readily accepted, Tammy viewed it as charity and said she didn't ask for it. Rhonda was hurt as it was unconditional kindness on her part; as a result, an old friendship disintegrated.

Rhonda and Jay realized their mistake was not setting down house rules. They assumed common courtesy would exist on all sides, but not everyone thinks the same way. Assumptions were made, and that is what created problems.

If you are extending an invitation to someone that may compromise your peace of mind and the normalcy in your life, make sure you have considered what long-term effect this may have on everyone involved. People support the person closest to them and can't (or aren't willing) to see bad behavior. In the end, conflict arises and relationships are compromised. House rules or boundaries need to be discussed and put in place before living arrangements are disrupted.

Define the expectations for all parties involved at the start of any arrangement. If any party can't live with them, then it is better not to get into a situation that may lead to hard feelings. Being considerate of other people's schedules and respecting their space as a visitor is common courtesy for most of us, but not all of us. If you are the person that created the problem and/or the misunderstanding, it is helpful if you accept some of the responsibility for what happened. That could save a friendship in the end. If you can't be accountable for your part, rarely is anything salvageable.

If you are generous to a fault, it is important that you are careful with your generosity and that you are not blinded by your own desire to be generous. It's not a matter of changing who you are but rather creating an awareness about who deserves your generosity.

The other part of this is if you are constantly extending generosity to people, it may be filling an empty spot inside you, and that may need to be examined so that you don't get hurt when the result is not what you anticipated. Figure out what the empty spot needs, and fill it in a more productive way.

Your Instant Insights...

- If you are extending an invitation to someone that may compromise your peace of mind and the normalcy in your life, make sure you have considered what long-term effects this may have on everyone involved.

- Define the expectations for all parties involved at the start of any arrangement. If any party can't live with them, then it is better not to get into a situation that may lead to hard feelings.

- If you are generous to a fault, it is important that you are careful with your generosity and that you are not blinded by your own desire to be generous.

Significant Others

They say opposites attract and that would certainly be the case with Len and Lucy. When they first met, there was much laughter with a dash of lighthearted sarcasm sprinkled in. As they spent time together, it was apparent they had the same values. Family was important to both of them, as were trust, loyalty, and respect.

Len and Lucy eventually married, and outside sources tested the strength of their marriage several times. Had they not understood that each had the other's back, they may not have made it over some of the hurdles. While they watched most relationships around them implode, they stayed strong. The family around them fell away—some divorced, some died—but still, through the disappointment and the tears, they were there for each other. It wasn't always easy, but the one thing they could hang on to was that they could count on each other.

Life is never stagnant, so all you can be sure of is change. During those tough times, you can blame each other, or you can remain committed through the storms together. The defining moment for Len and Lucy was when they decided they would stick together even though everything around them changed. Len took seriously the marriage vow to "forsake all others." He lived by those words and always had Lucy's back.

Len and Lucy always knew they thought differently about things, but it wasn't until they decided to take the Myers-Briggs personality profile that they realized they were complete opposites. In a four-letter description, one was an "I" while the other an "E"; one was an "S" while the other an "N"; one was a "T" while the other an "F"; and lastly, one was a "P" while the other a "J." Without going into a lengthy explanation about the types, what this meant was that in every instance, they reacted in different ways, their thought processes were different, and their views were different. (Information can easily be found about Myers-Briggs or MBTI by searching online.)

Understanding our significant other's personality type—the ways that they respond and react to and handle situations—can go far to strengthen and keep a relationship together. We can't expect someone to always hold the same vision we have, and accepting each other's differences can be like opening a window to a different view. It can be an awakening.

Opposites may attract, but when you are so very different at your core, at your approach to life, it takes work. You also need a lot of understanding along with compassion for how each person deals with life situations and even daily life to stay strong.

No one said being in a relationship would be easy, and only you can decide if it is worth the work. Len and Lucy decided it was, and even through stressful and challenging times, if they didn't believe they had each other's back, they may not have made it. When they got close to throwing it all away, the one constant was they always knew they could count on the other no matter what the world threw at them. There is a peace in that like no other and a strength that could survive anything.

If we were all the same, our potential for growth in relationships would be nonexistent. You can learn from each other, and hearing someone else's opinion can be enlightening. Brushing off someone's ideas could be a great disservice to yourself—you might miss an opportunity to learn something new. Cherish the differences and grow together. It can make for a long, strong relationship full of new and interesting ideas.

Your Instant Insights...

- Understanding our significant other's personality type—the ways that they respond and react to and handle situations—can go far to strengthen and keep a relationship together.

- We are all different, and expecting a person to react the same as you in all situations is a recipe for disaster. Taking time to understand, without judgment or criticism, why they react differently makes your connection stronger. No one wants to be judged because they don't have the same opinion or reaction that you do.

- Brushing off someone's ideas could be a great disservice to yourself—you might miss an opportunity to learn something new. Cherish the differences and grow together.

Difficult Siblings

Two sisters, Lisa and Marie, have never been close. Marie is the eldest, and from a very early age, she just did not seem to like Lisa, who would have been happy to have a close relationship with her sister, but it was not to be. Lisa could do nothing right no matter how hard she tried. She was criticized, minimized, brushed off or worse, she was simply ignored. When Lisa praised Marie, she was met with a sarcastic or derogatory retort. Lisa could never figure out what she did wrong, and sadly, she never would.

Conversation with Marie was impossible as Marie was judgmental and always had to be right. Marie had no interest in anything Lisa had to say. She was not pleasant to be around, but that didn't stop Lisa from trying to make their relationship work. Over time, however, it became more and more difficult to keep trying. Lisa tried to accept that this was the ways things were going to be. It takes two people to work on a relationship for it to improve, and it appeared Marie had no interest in making any effort at all.

For the sake of family, Lisa was sociable but kept her distance. She spent her time at family functions closer to the people she enjoyed being around and avoided having much contact with Marie. It was tolerable but unpleasant as it made Lisa act like someone different from her real self.

The defining moment in their relationship came years later. Lisa witnessed Marie's bad behavior in a way that sealed the deal for her. Marie seemed to have a way of trying to control others, and when she couldn't, that person would no longer be on her good side and she would start mistreating them. Marie was bad-tempered and seemed to be angry at the world for some unknown reason.

Lisa recognized that she wasn't the only target of Marie's bad temper, even though she was probably the most often hit. She reached a point where she really didn't care for her sister, so gaining her approval mattered less. With that realization, it was much easier to be around Marie. She knew the approval was never coming, so she gave up trying to create a relationship. It took a long time to get there, but she was trying to find peace. Without peace, the struggle would continue forever, and it just wasn't worth the energy it took to try to build a relationship alone.

You cannot change a relationship if only one person in the relationship feels the need to change something. If you choose to be in situations where that person is present, you need to find a way to coexist. Recognizing that you may not be the problem goes a long way to helping you be comfortable in their presence, but it is hard not to be affected. Look at the person's behavior, and notice if it's just you that's being mistreated. If it's not, then chances are you are not the problem. You may just be the safest and easiest target for that person. For your own sanity, you have to look for the way that works for you, whether it is ignoring that person or removing yourself from close proximity to them.

Beating your head against a brick wall, trying to understand why this person treats you badly, is futile. You will never know unless you can have a conversation about it, and even then there is no guarantee that you will find the answer you seek. The other person may become defensive or argumentative, which may create a bigger barrier between you. Find a way to accept what is and move forward, even if you don't have the answers you want.

Removing yourself from the situation is always a solution, but there may be reasons that you don't want to be away from the group or family; that makes it harder to walk away. Being there to see the next generation grow up or being present as a family member's health declines while there is still time or still recognition are among the many reasons one would choose to continue to be in the presence of someone who treats you badly. If you have to be there, protect yourself as best you can, and enjoy the company of the rest of the group. It's amazing how easily you can be lost in the shuffle if you really try. If it is too difficult, then finding safer ways to spend time with those you want to see is better than putting yourself in a potential war zone.

Continuous anger brewing under the surface is bound to eventually explode, and you don't want to be anywhere near it when it blows. Determining the cost to you could help make your decisions easier.

Your Instant Insights...

- You cannot change a relationship if only one person in the relationship feels the need to change something. Look at the person's behavior, and notice if it's just you that's being mistreated. If it's not, then chances are you are not the problem.

- Find a way to accept what is and move forward, even if you don't have the answers you want.

- Continuous anger brewing under the surface is bound to eventually explode, and you don't want to be anywhere near it when it blows. Determining the cost to you could help make your decisions easier.

Blameless Siblings

Jack had always been a little bit different. He could be kind and generous, but at times there was something off, like he was missing some of the filtering mechanisms one should have picked up along the way to adulthood. Jack was intelligent, but he was missing a link to common sense. He lived for the day, which is good in some ways, but it was detrimental to him as he didn't seem to think about what would happen tomorrow.

When it came to finances, his life was a mess. He always expected someone else to take care of him, and for most of his life, somebody did. Eventually there came a time when there really was no one else that could help. Money was the tool that would solve all his problems, and if you couldn't provide that, you were no longer of use to him. It affected everyone close to him, and they all struggled with it.

He was obviously suffering from some form of mental disturbance and was either not being treated or being treated incorrectly. A doctor could only treat him if Jack came clean and was aware of his behavior, but that was not the case. Everyone else was to blame for what went wrong in his life. Nothing was ever his fault.

It was difficult to step in because he was not a stupid man, but he was unaware of his behaviours and didn't seem to care how they affected others. He felt some paranoia that everyone was out to get him, so he laughed at or got angry with anyone who tried to help in another way. Family members were concerned and helpless all at the same time.

As he aged, his inability to keep the filter in check made it more and more difficult for anyone to reside with him or be around him. He continued to move every few months, which disturbed everyone that cared about him. In his view, the only way anyone cared for him was by providing him with money. If family continued to do so, it would be to their own detriment, but that was something he could never see, something he never tried to comprehend. Family members had jobs, so in his mind they had money. He wouldn't even think about the expenses they needed to pay.

Eventually, if you didn't assist Jack financially, he would just shut you out of his life. It was very difficult for his family to be tossed aside, but it was a stalemate. If you didn't have the financial resources, you no longer held any value for him, regardless of how you were connected. Sadly, this was the defining moment in any relationship with him. It was his choice that closed people out of his life, and there was not much anyone could do about it.

It was sad, but the family had to find a way to come to terms with it. After a time, no one had a way to even contact Jack. Members of the family no longer knew where he lived. His phone was disconnected regularly, and he would have a new number that no one knew. It was hard dealing with that reality. It was emotionally devastating for many of his family members. There was such a feeling of helplessness within the family because Jack would just turn his back on everyone. In his mind, he felt the family had turned their backs on him, but that wasn't the case at all. No amount of explanation could change his mind.

If you are no longer part of someone's life because you stopped giving them money, there is not much you can do about that. If financial support is no longer something you can provide and you are tossed aside because of it, it's their choice, not yours. You have to find peace knowing you haven't walked away and would help in other ways; if that is not acceptable though, then your hands are tied.

It's hard to be in a situation where you are concerned someone you love may become homeless and you don't know where they are or how to reach them. As difficult as it is, you have to realize it is their right to walk away. It's no different from an addict. It is their choice to continue in their lifestyle because they don't want to hear what anyone has to say. Although it doesn't make it any easier, there truly is little, if anything, you can do. They have to want help, but if they don't think there is anything wrong with them, you are fighting an uphill battle. Treatment for someone who doesn't believe anything is wrong with them is next to impossible. There is a gap in handling these types of medical situations, so you stay stuck and helpless in assisting them.

If someone only valued you as a means to money, what value did you really have in their life? It's painful and terrifying to not know where a loved one may be, but we can't make their choices for them. We can only pray and hope they are safe and trust that someday they will find their way back or their way to some peace in their lives.

Your Instant Insights...

- If financial support is no longer something you can provide and you are tossed aside because of it, it's their choice, not yours. You have to find peace knowing you haven't walked away and would help in other ways. If that is not acceptable though, then your hands are tied.

- As difficult as it is, you have to realize it is their right to walk away.

- If someone only values you as a means to money, what value did you really have in their life?

Youth and Broken Trust

Joe was a good Catholic boy. He was taught to respect his elders and those in authority. As a child of an immigrant family in the United States, he believed that this was the land of opportunity. As a child, he trusted his parents and anyone in power completely and without question. That was the way he was raised.

At the young age of ten, Joe was being taught civics in school. He was learning about the government and things like the Senate. During that time, an incident about some spying over Russia was being discussed in the news. The president of the United States steadfastly denied having any part in this spying incident.

One day after school, Joe came home and turned on the television. There was the president on the black-and-white television admitting that he lied and that the United States was in fact spying on Russia. As a young man, Joe could not believe that "his president" would lie to him. This was his new home and "his America," and he couldn't understand or believe that this would happen in his newfound country. He never forgot the shock and disappointment he felt.

When serving his church as an altar boy at the age of eleven, Joe was standing at the top of a set of stairs. At the bottom, he heard voices and recognized those of the Father Superior and the choirmaster. He heard the Father say "those God-damned kids," and Joe felt as if a knife went into his heart.

The words shook this eleven-year-old boy to the core. As a child who was taught respect and who held both men in very high regard, Joe was devastated. He had actually been thinking of entering the priesthood, but at that moment, the feeling of deception from those in whom he had put all his trust and faith was traumatic for this young boy, and it changed him.

One day at recess at Catholic school, a boy came up to Joe and kicked him in the genitals. The boys had seen this on TV as a funny prank, much like The Three Stooges poking eyes. Unfortunately, Joe could barely move afterwards.

The school bell rang, and the playground monitor came up to Joe and tried to hurry him up to go back into the school. Joe tried to tell her what happened, but she just wanted him to get back into the school because recess was over. He tried and tried to explain that he was injured, but she didn't seem to care. There was never any discussions of the incident, even though Joe was seriously hurt.

Once again, Joe was denied the sense of protection he thought he had while at the school. The lack of concern from those that were in charge and were supposed to watch over their youth was nonexistent, which once again destroyed the feeling of trust for Joe.

Then there was a fourth occurrence at summer day camp. A group of kids went swimming in a pool that was overseen by a lifeguard. One boy, obviously thinking it would be funny, tried to strangle Joe underwater. Joe could barely breathe, and when the boy finally let go, Joe sputtered and coughed his way to the top. He went to the lifeguard to tell him that someone tried to choke and drown him, but again Joe was brushed aside and told to stay out of the water. How could any young boy who had suffered these circumstances grow up to respect those in power?

Any one of these situations would be a defining moment in a young boy's life, but lump them together and his view of authority would certainly have been formed—and not in a good way. Think of what that does to one's idea of authority as you go through life. It would take a fairly significant figure to be able to restore that trust in this young man's soul.

Respect is respect, regardless of your age. If you are a person in charge, disregarding a child who has brought forth a concern will only make the child feel dismissed and that authority cannot be trusted. That is probably not the impression you want to make on a young mind. Just because someone is young doesn't mean they don't have a legitimate complaint.

If a child's sense of safety is wrapped up in trusting that there are adults that will protect them, then it is the responsibility of those adults to keep them safe and ensure they are protected or, at the very least, heard. If they can't, then they should allow someone else to be in the position.

People are affected by what others do. Be careful not to leave scars on another because you can't be bothered to spend the time to address a situation. Young minds form opinions, and if they are hurt or ignored, they come to question their own value.

These are the types of things that start a person on the path of feeling "unworthy," and that is a long, hard battle to fight your way back to feeling "worthy." Remember that these are the adults of our future. Teach them well, and don't let them feel like they don't matter ... because they do.

Your Instant Insights...

- Respect is respect, regardless of your age.

- If a child's sense of safety is wrapped up in trusting that there are adults that will protect them, then it is the responsibility of those adults to keep them safe and ensure they are protected or, at the very least, heard.

- Be careful not to leave scars on another because you can't be bothered to spend the time to address a situation.

Male Friendships

As they grew up, brothers James and Matt didn't spend a lot of time together. They were close in age, but their interests and circles of friends were very different so their lives were fairly separate.

There was an incident where Matt was injured while trying to help James. The injury never healed properly, and it affected Matt's movements for the rest of his life. Matt was also emotionally hurt by the fact that James never once expressed any concern about Matt's injury. It cemented a rift between them that went on for many years.

One day, Matt, who was not a drinker, had a few too many and decided to phone James and tell him what he thought. This surprised James, which upset Matt even more. After that, the relationship started to take a step toward healing, but it took some time for them to learn to appreciate each other as brothers.

The defining moment that changed the relationship came when James became ill. Realizing time is precious and that he really didn't have many family members left, James started to contact Matt on a more regular basis. They started to talk more often and visit each other on occasion. In their own way, they started to show more concern for each other, and they grew closer.

Grant and Ryan experienced a similar parting of the ways. Ryan had been absent from Grant's life for a few years, and it wasn't until Grant became suddenly ill that Ryan resurfaced. Ryan was the one that made the effort, and although it was hard at first, after a few difficult discussions, they found a way to become closer.

A third party had created the rift, and Ryan had only heard one side of the story. In order to make an informed decision going forward, both sides had to be heard; as difficult as they were for Ryan to hear, only then would everyone involved know if moving forward was going to be possible. Thankfully it was, and a relationship was restored.

Knowing only one side of the story doesn't give you a proper viewpoint to be able to assess what really happened, thereby enabling you to make up your own mind about things.

Friends for over thirty years, John and Carl were separated because of a complete misunderstanding. Again, alcohol gave John the courage to call Carl and try to deal with the situation. They spoke for the first time in many years. It was a beginning, and they continued to speak. A few years later when they finally had a chance to see each other in person, both cried and regretted the time they had lost. They had been great friends and let a silly misunderstanding fuel pain and a separation between them because they didn't talk it out.

Many men deal with things differently than women and seem to find it much harder to talk things through. However, as witnessed above, once they do, relationships can be restored.

If a relationship needs healing, waiting until an illness shows up is taking a chance. Although sometimes it's the "almost" losing someone that can make you realize you want them in your life, an illness could result in a death, taking with it the chance to reconcile and heal a relationship. So be careful not to wait until it's too late because regrets can live forever.

Many estranged relationships result from miscommunication or misunderstandings. If the relationship is worth saving, it is worth taking a stab at finding a way to make it better or finding a solution. If you're not sure what happened, you can at least get to the bottom of it. In the end, you will know you tried, and if it doesn't work, you will have no regrets. If you don't try, you will never know.

If we were meant to be alone, I don't believe there would be so many of us. Don't isolate yourself on principle. Hanging on to your principles can be a cold, lonely place to hang out. In the end, it really is not worth standing on principle if talking can mend the fences and renew a good friendship or relationship.

LESIA ZABLOCKIJ

Your Instant Insights...

- Be careful not to wait until it's too late because regrets can live forever.

- If the relationship is worth saving, it is worth taking a stab at finding a way to make it better or finding a solution.

- It really is not worth standing on principle if talking can mend the fences and renew a good friendship or relationship.

Lost Souls

Tracey was a spirited young lady with eyes that sparkled brilliantly when she smiled. She had a zest for life and enjoyed being around people. Because of some troubling family events, she somehow lost her sparkle and began a downward spiral into apathy and with apathy came hoarding. She felt she had lost everything and held on to anything she could. She lost her way and dug herself into a rut that was difficult for her to escape. She spoke to counsellors, worked with a coach, and tried many other things as well. Although Tracey understood her situation, it appeared that she could not find the energy or motivation to take steps to improve it.

Tracey was a highly sensitive person, and although she tried to appear tough, she took everything in, which damaged her self-confidence. She was surrounded by dysfunction, and it appeared to make her think she was "flawed," which she was not. Tracey did not want to offend anyone, so in the end, she tried to please everyone else to the exclusion of herself. She was close to her mother, but unfortunately her mother questioned so many of Tracey's decisions that it was agonizing for her to make a decision on her own. She lacked direction and felt so unsure ... and the years rolled by.

Alexis was concerned and cared very much for Tracey's welfare. Alexis tried many ways to get through to Tracey, including attending meetings with medical professionals in support. Unfortunately, Alexis was at cross-purposes with Tracey's mother, who would quietly sabotage anything Alexis tried to do. Her mother refused to look inward; consequently, the things that Tracey suffered with could not be addressed.

Because of this and her loyalty to her mother, Tracey remained stuck. There was a codependent element to their relationship that was evident to many others, but not to them. They cared for each other but also used each other to fill time. It was easy, and they didn't have to put much effort into not being alone as they were often together, filling the emptiness for each other. Alexis worried about the time when Tracey would be left alone without that crutch to lean on.

The defining moment for Alexis was when she realized the stumbling block she was facing was because of their codependent nature. She knew that until Tracey saw things more clearly, there was no way to break through the wall around those two individuals. It didn't matter how much Alexis cared for Tracey, she would never be able to break the codependent part of the relationship she had with her mother, even if it was for Tracey's own good. Alexis had to be at peace with it and try to be there for Tracey when she reached out to her, knowing she could only reach so far. She had to find a way to cope with the situation so that it didn't hurt Tracey or herself.

It doesn't matter how much you care about a person; it doesn't matter if you see that their life could be so much better. If they don't want to take steps to have a better life, it is their choice and their life. You have to step back and allow their life to take whatever shape it needs to and be there if or when required. It can be very painful to watch, but you can't push your agenda onto them.

Even though you only want what you think is best for another individual, you can't want it for them more than they want it for themselves. They need to step up, and until they do, you can't do it for them as you will only get so far. You may get frustrated, but you have to be able to let them guide their own lives. Sometimes all you can do is hope and pray for the best.

In an effort to preserve a relationship, you need to be careful not to push your ideas, even if the individual keeps saying they are ready for help. If they continue to refuse to take action, it is futile to keep trying to make someone else do what you think they should. They will come to it in their own time, or they won't. You just need to care about them without judgment. After all, love is supposed to be unconditional.

Your Instant Insights...

- It doesn't matter how much you care about a person; it doesn't matter if you see that their life could be so much better. If they don't want to take steps to have a better life, it is their choice and their life.

- Even though you only want what you think is best for another individual, you can't want it for them more than they want it for themselves.

- In an effort to preserve a relationship, you need to be careful not to push your ideas, even if the individual keeps saying they are ready for help.

Mentors

It was Laura's first job in the big city, working in a prestigious downtown firm. It was exciting and scary. George was her boss, and he was meticulous. He was a perfectionist and insisted on the highest standard of output from Laura, which, in time, she provided. She enjoyed the work and enjoyed the firm.

A few years later she was offered a paralegal position. When she decided to accept the position, George asked her to reconsider. He had also decided to leave but at that point didn't know where or when. The bigger part of the equation was that he wasn't sure if he could take Laura with him, and that was the deciding factor to make Laura leave. There were no guarantees if she stayed, so she took the position that advanced her career.

Over the years, George invited Laura to return a couple times, but for whatever reason the timing wasn't quite right. Several years later, the opportunity came up again. The timing was right, and Laura was ready to return to work for George again, but George wanted to have a bit of an interview first. Imagine!

The interview quickly ended after George asked, "What have you done lately that would be of assistance to me?" Laura responded, "I can type," and that was the end of that interview. Anything else she was confident she could learn and so was George.

Laura happily returned. They were a great team, working hard and taking time to spend with others in the office socially. George made her part of other things he was involved in, such as elections, the theater, and cultural events.

After a number of years, the economy turned, the work slowed down, and the ideology of the firm started to change. The big deals were declining, and those were the things Laura enjoyed the most. Laura became bored and was approached about another position, which she decided to check out. She was hired, so once again she was leaving. It was a sad few weeks as she was leaving the firm but did not necessarily want to stop working for George.

On her last day, George left early, avoiding the last-minute farewell, saying his goodbyes to Laura in his office. He put his hands on both sides of her face, kissed her goodbye, and said, "We will talk."

Over the next twenty-five years, they had only one conversation. George passed away in his sleep much too young. It was totally unexpected as he was a healthy, active man who took care of himself. The news devastated Laura. He was an integral part of forming who she was in her career, and she was saddened that she hadn't told him.

It wasn't until George passed that Laura realized that George had really been her mentor. Laura always assumed that one day their paths would cross again. It was not to be, and that was a bit of a shock to Laura. She always knew he had trained her to become so organized and to stay on top of her workload. George taught her to be just as painstakingly thorough as he was, which was definitely an asset as she advanced her career. She took pride in her work because that was what George had taught her. When she reached that defining moment, she realized she could no longer tell him because it was too late. She hoped that somehow he knew.

Never wait until it's too late to tell someone what an impact they have had on your life. All too often we miss our chance to express that gratitude, and it could be so meaningful to both sides to have it expressed.

Most people take pride in their work, but if a mentor nurtured that in you, even if you were unaware of it at the time, it is definitely something to be appreciated once you realize it. Perhaps you should pass that on to that mentor.

Sometimes when you are in the middle of a situation at work, it is hard to know whether to stay or go. We all grow, and there comes a time when it is just time to move on. It may not have anything to do with your current boss, but instead the philosophy or strategies of the organization in general. Only you can decide when it is the right time to move on. All you can do is make sure your reasons are true and not a story you have convinced yourself is true. Sometimes it's just time to go.

Your Instant Insights...

- Never wait until it's too late to tell someone what an impact they have had on your life.

- Most people take pride in their work, but if a mentor nurtured that in you, even if you were unaware of it at the time, it is definitely something to be appreciated once you realize it. Perhaps you should pass that on to that mentor.

- Only you can decide when it is the right time to move on. All you can do is make sure your reasons are true and not a story you have convinced yourself is true.

Workplaces

As a young career woman, Vicky decided to leave her job and take on a new responsibility in a more senior position. It was only her third year working in her chosen field, so she was quite excited to be given the opportunity at such a young age. Unfortunately, it was a strange experience to say the least.

Although the company was a blend of many individuals, most were of a certain religious belief, and Vicky was an outsider. In fact, it really wasn't a good fit at all. Unfortunately, she didn't know that until she started working there.

The office itself was beautiful. She had a lovely work area and current equipment, but she soon discovered that all that shines may not be what it seems. The old adage "don't judge a book by its cover" came to her mind.

Vicky had a minor health issue that she divulged when she was interviewed. A few months into her employment, she was called into one of the partners' offices and questioned about it. Vicky reminded him that she made them aware of it before they hired her.

A while later, a new employee was hired, and during conversations in the coffee room, she mentioned that during her interview, she was asked if she was going to have any more children. After that question, she was asked what method of birth control she used. Vicky was beside herself. Any self-respecting business should know how inappropriate this type of questioning was, but they asked anyway. It was unbelievable. Who was she working for at this new office? This was a defining moment for her, and she started to look for a new job.

Vicky felt increasingly uncomfortable, but because she was young and had been trained by the company, she felt an obligation to stay. She even refused another job offer through some ridiculous sense of loyalty. That loyalty would turn out to be very one-sided.

After a few months, she was called into a partner's office and fired. She excused herself quickly as she had a job interview to attend. An hour and a half later she had a new job and started work the following Monday at her new job. It was a blessing in so many ways.

It would have been nice to say that was the end of that chapter in Vicky's life, but it wasn't. She filed a Labor Board claim that she had to fight for almost a year going forward; she took on the company for wrongdoing.

They touted their religious beliefs, but in this circumstance they weren't above fabricating information—they just plain lied. In the end, Vicky won her claim and the money she was owed as she was able to prove their lies.

It was never about anything but principle for Vicky. She hadn't lost any money as she started a new job immediately. She just knew that she had done nothing wrong, that there was no reason for this treatment, and that she was not afraid to fight them. Vicky's few years' work experience had taught her something about standing up for herself. She had documentation to disprove every silly accusation they made, and the day before the hearing was scheduled, her money was paid and the claim closed. This experience taught her that you shouldn't fear standing up for yourself when you know you are not at fault.

Be careful about where you place your loyalty— and with whom you place it. If you are unsure if they are worthy, be careful to protect yourself as best you can until you are sure. If you are never sure, keep your options open and safeguard yourself and your career as best you can. Always make sure your best interest is being served and your resume is current.

If you know you have nothing to be ashamed of and you have done nothing to deserve being treated badly, you don't have to put up with it. It doesn't matter that people have more power than you. If you know you have done nothing wrong and have proof that they did, you need to take a stand for yourself or you may never be able to do so in the future.

Standing up for yourself when you know you are not at fault is not only a courageous move but also a move that is necessary for your own self-confidence. Each circumstance has to be examined, but if you have been screwed out of something that is rightfully yours, such as money owed, you have a right to stand up and fight for it. After all, if you don't, nobody else will.

Your Instant Insights...

- Always make sure your best interest is being served and your resume is current.

- If you know you have nothing to be ashamed of and you have done nothing to deserve being treated badly, you don't have to put up with it.

- Standing up for yourself when you know you are not at fault is not only a courageous move but also a move that is necessary for your own self-confidence.

All About You!

I have learned and witnessed in so many ways that if you don't have a good relationship with yourself, all your other relationships will suffer. You might be wondering what I mean by that, or you might be thinking that your relationship with yourself is just fine. However, if you are having trouble with any kind of relationship, you may need to look inward first.

All of those "self" issues come up for a reason: self-worth, self-esteem, self-awareness, self-confidence, self-acceptance, self-love, self-care, self-doubt, and self-respect, to name a few. Most important is self-love.

If you learn to love and accept yourself, warts and all, you will be kinder if you screw up—which we all do. If you love yourself, you can be forgiving with yourself and then with others. It's the old ripple effect all over again. It truly does have to start with you.

If you carry something with you because of a mistake you made or something you did in the past, how is it possible to forgive that in someone else? No one gave us the rule book when we got here. We had to sink or swim, and I am sure we have all done a little of both. Loving and accepting yourself allows you to have that same openness toward other human beings in your life.

Life is always about the baggage we collect along the way and continue to carry with us. Baggage adds nothing to our life; it just weighs us down. What's more surprising is that the thoughts or beliefs inside the baggage are most likely past their expiry date—they no longer matter, but we still carry them with us.

It may have served us once and even protected us, but what if that's no longer the case? The baggage that you carry may have kept you safe at one time, but maybe it's time to take out the trash. If someone hurt you and you have never been able to forgive yourself for not seeing it beforehand, how will that affect your relationships going forward? If you have been hurt by someone, don't make yourself stop trusting out of fear you will be hurt again. It might just be time to stop making others pay for something that someone else did to you.

The first step is always forgiving yourself. If we could see the hand we are dealt from beginning to end, we wouldn't have risked or gambled with our decisions. We would know the outcome at the start, but where's the magic in that? We make mistakes. We make wrong choices, and we end up getting hurt. We make those decisions with the information that is available to us at the time, so blaming ourselves is futile.

We come into this world loving and accepting everyone. If that has changed for you somewhere along the way, it's time to figure out when the armor went up and why. Figure out when you needed to feel safe and why you suddenly felt different inside. Your behavior toward others, and especially toward yourself, may be damaging, and it's time to change that.

Forgive yourself, forgive others, and learn to love yourself again. What may have protected you once can now be hurting you, and it's important to recognize that these outdated beliefs are just that—outdated—and they need to be changed. That is the defining moment that can create a better future for you.

Finding the defining moment when you lost touch with that person (you) that only knew how to love is a big step toward a strong relationship with yourself. You can then see the beginning of other healthy relationships moving forward.

Being able to forgive and accept that you may not be perfect and that you have made mistakes doesn't mean you are a bad person. It just means you are human, and as humans, we make mistakes. We need to be able to move on from those mistakes and allow others to do so as well. We only learn from our mistakes, so ease up on yourself. Reflect, learn, and make new choices now that you have more awareness and better information.

Once you have learned to love and forgive yourself, you will find it easier to love and forgive others. It's time to stop making yourself or someone else continue to pay for a mistake made a long time ago. You wouldn't want someone to do that to you. None of us are perfect, but we can all learn from our mistakes and become better people. Open your eyes and then open your heart. It's all that matters in the end.

Your Instant Insights...

- Finding the defining moment when you lost touch with that person (you) that only knew how to love is a big step toward a strong relationship with yourself.

- We only learn from our mistakes, so ease up on yourself. Reflect, learn, and make new choices now that you have more awareness and better information.

- Once you have learned to love and forgive yourself, you will find it easier to love and forgive others.

About the Author

Lesia Zablockij considers herself a life "pathologist," a personality profiler, and a mindset mentor. In her search to uncover her purpose, she discovered a love of teaching and helping others. She wants to help them celebrate the best parts of themselves while honoring the "not so pretty" parts and finding peace with both.

Lesia's dream has been to run intimate retreats by creating a safe place for people to explore and understand what they really want in life and why they don't have it. The group workshops she currently facilitates provide a version of that safe place so that people can embrace and let go of what they need to in their lives.

The groups form a community that so many feel no longer exists in their lives. We all learn from each other. All members have the freedom to express themselves without fear and to explore new possibilities. It's like filling your lungs with fresh air.

Since embarking on this road over ten years ago, Lesia has received the following training and certifications:

> Associate Certified Coach @ ICF (International Coach Federation)
>
> Now What?™ 90 Days to a New Life Direction Facilitator

Grief Recovery Specialist (The Grief Recovery Method®)

Certified Life Coach

Success Principles™ Coach Graduate (Jack Canfield)

Success Team Leader (Barbara Sher – SherSuccess Teams)

Career Counsellor

And she is certified in the following personality profiling tools:

Myers-Briggs™

The Print® (The Paul Hertz Group)

Core Temperament Essentials®

Sacred Money Archetypes™

Human Needs Assessment

Enneagram (in progress)

Connect with the Author

Websites:
www.SoulFireCafe.com
www.AlteringMindsets.com

Email:
alteringmindsets@gmail.com

Social Media:
Facebook: https://www.facebook.com/groups/alteringmindsets/

LinkedIn: https://ca.linkedin.com/in/lesia-zablockij-acc-401b4b99

Other Books by the Lesia Zablockij

Soul Fire Café – Making Peace with the One in the Mirror

About Crescendo Publishing

Crescendo Publishing is a boutique-style, concierge VIP publishing company assisting entrepreneurs with writing, publishing, and promoting their books for the purposes of lead-generation and achieving global platform growth, then monetizing it for even more income opportunities.

Check out some of our latest best-selling AuthorPreneurs at
http://CrescendoPublishing.com/new-authors

About the Instant Insights™
Book Series

The *Instant Insights™ Book Series* is a fact-only, short-read, book series written by EXPERTS in very specialized categories. These high-value, high-quality books can be produced in ONLY 6-8 weeks, from concept to launch, in BOTH PRINT & eBOOK Formats!

This book series is FOR YOU if:

- You are an expert in your niche or area of specialty

- You want to write a book to position yourself as an expert

- You want YOUR OWN book – NOT a chapter in someone else's book

- You want to have a book to give to people when you're speaking at events or simply networking

- You want to have it available quickly

- You don't have the time to invest in writing a 200-page full book

- You don't have a ton of money to invest in the production of a full book – editing, cover design, interior layout, best-seller promotion

- You don't have a ton of time to invest in finding quality contractors for the production of your book – editing, cover design, interior layout, best-seller promotion

For more information on how you can become an *Instant Insights™* author, visit **www.InstantInsightsBooks.com**

More Books in the
Instant Insight Series

A Time Management System *for* Creative Entrepreneurs

Branding & Website Essentials *for* Entrepreneurs

How to Create & Build a Successful Beauty Business

Organizing Your Workspace *for* a Productivity Boost

How to be a Happy & Prosperous CEO

Taking Your Business from Start Up to Thrive in 45 Days

7 Strategies *for* Raising Calm, Inspired, & Successful Children

Creating a Solid, Lasting Connection with Your Kids

12 Leadership Powers *for* Successful Women

Motivation: Your Master Key to Success & Riches!

Performance Power: Clarity, Confidence, & Joy

Practical Natural Healing Tips *for* Vibrant Living

The Art of Selling to a Woman

Unconventional Methods *for* Writing a Best Selling Book

Defining Moments with Family, Friends, & More

Building a Conflict-Proof Relationship

CrescendoPublishing.com